The Stance To Get Elected

By Parker Bono

Also By Parker Bono

The Stance To Lead

As always,
I dedicate this book to the American
people and those who fight and fought
for my rights.

Contents

Dedication   2

Introduction   6

FEDERAL

1. **The Background**   8

2. **The Announcement**   10

3. **Staff And Advisors**
   46

4. **The Media**   52

5. **Funding**   56

6. **The Primary Rallies**   58

7. **The First Debate**   68

8. **The First Primary/Caucus**   69

9. **Future Primaries/Caucuses**   70

10. **Future Debates And Quorums** 71

11. **Getting The Nomination**   72

The Stance To Get Elected

12. The Convention   75

13. The General Election Rallies   90

14. The Presidential Debates   91

15. The Ad Campaign   93

16. Election Day   94

17. Victory Speech   95

STATE

18. The Background   100

19. The Announcement   101

20. The Primary   111

21. The Ad Campaign   112

22. Election Day   113

23. Victory Speech   114

MISCELLANEOUS

24. Get Politically Involved   118

Introduction

The Stance To Get Elected is a book that is about the essence of winning, but particularly in elections. In the book, I explain how I plan to run my campaign, gather funds, and how to win the presidency. I also tell how I plan on getting elected as Governor of Pennsylvania. Finally, I also explain how you yourself can get involved politically.

If one is to get elected to these positions, they must have many aspects but the most important ones are a background, name recognition, and love from the people.

I will achieve a background in Politics as that will be my job for the rest of my life. I will be a public servant. I will be loved by the people as I will do what is right. I will grow, develop, and improve whatever city I reside upon as a city council member and mayor. I also will help the district in which I represent in the House Of Representatives. I will also run an excellent campaign to be governor of the state I am a resident of and ultimately win the people's vote and be elected President of the United States in 2040. This plan is outlined in this book, as well as how I shall achieve the plans.

I decided to write this book since I love politics and I have a plan for everything. I capitalize on every situation, and you should to. This book means a lot to me, and it is basically a blueprint for my future, as well as our country. I explain how I plan on winning and I also explain how we as a country will as well. You don't have to win in politics to be a winner. Millions of Americans may not be winners yet but if they have the mindset of one, they surely will be soon.

I believe everyone has something in life to give and I would love to see everyone reach their potential. I however have seen many very talented and brilliant people not do what they are easily capable of. This is called laziness. The trait of laziness has a direct correlation to failure. This book explains how to win, as well as how I plan on doing it in future elections, and in general. If you read this book, you will benefit as you will obtain new knowledge. You also will see my plans that I ensure you will occur successfully.

Chapter One
The Background

"I walk slowly but I never walk backward."
-Abraham Lincoln

If one is to get elected President of the United States, they must have a very good background. I myself will have graduated from Political Science Penn State University with a degree in . I then will run for City Council (2022), Mayor (2026), House of Representatives (2030), Governor (2034), and President (2040). My job throughout my life will be a public servant. I will provide the people with a government run by them. Nobody will be able to buy me out because I will do the right thing for the country. The jobs I will acquire in the beginning of my career and the jobs I get later on will have a domino effect on the next as each new job will be beneficial towards my future.

Another item I will be able to put on my resume is the fact that I will have eliminated the debt in every location and district I resided over. My eyes would next be on the U.S. National Debt. No sane person wants themselves, their spouse, and their children to each owe $61,500 just for living in the United States. I will run as a Republican throughout the course of my political career although I do have many independent views and common sense views such as enforcing law, eliminating the U.S. National Debt, job growth, etc. Basically, I will run as a Republican since I must pick one of the two major parties but I will actually be more of an independent.

To restate, I will graduate from Penn State University and I will have a career in politics. I will create a name for myself and I will become synonymous with victory. I will be an independent that successfully runs as a Republican. I believe that in the future I will have the necessary background to lead. I also believe I will win over the people, no matter my location, and I will be a political success.

Chapter Two
The Announcement

"We would all like to vote for the best man but he is never a candidate." -Kin Hubbard

---

After I create a background for myself in politics, I will announce my candidacy for President of the United States. My announcement speech will be approximately 5,000 words and will take about 45 minutes for me to read off of a teleprompter. I despise of the teleprompter but it is necessary at certain points in time to properly get your point across to the American people. My speech would be held on May 1, 2039, at Independence Hall in Pennsylvania. I should get approximately 7,500 people to show up for my speech, almost reaching the maximum capacity of Independence Hall (the place the Declaration Of Independence and the Constitution were written).

During my speech, I will speak out against my opponents and politicians in general, warn against associating with a political party, speak about ending the Federal Reserve, lay out my plan to end the National Debt within 8 years, immigration reform, my tax plan, problems with the world at the time and how I will do everything in my power to fix them, and much much more. Obviously, I can not predict the future by knowing what will happen in 22 years from now so I speak about things the way they are today. I would change this in my actual announcement speech, although it would be very similar.

Below is my speech announcing my candidacy for President of the United States.

"Thank you everyone for coming. That's a lot of people out there. Many thousands!

It is my great honor to be speaking here today at the location our nation was founded. When our nation was founded, the greatest leaders our country has ever seen came out and fought for liberty. I don't see that today. When our nation was founded, people knew their genders, people knew which bathroom to use, and people were willing to work relentlessly to form the system we have today. The system is perfect. It is the greatest thing the world has ever seen, and it is known as the American Experiment.

America was founded on the ideals that we wouldn't take anything from anyone. Britain attempted to tax us at an insane rate. In response we went to war. We were the underdogs but we won.

But this was back then. I don't see us winning as much as we should be today. We lose at trade, we lose at costs, we lose at the borders, and most importantly, we lose at the military. China is spending ¼ of what we are spending on the military yet they are growing their military at a quicker rate. Our government is one of the least efficient and effective in the world. If the federal government was put in charge of manufacturing iPhones, the price to make them would go up from $220 to $2,200, and our leaders are so stupid, they wouldn't change the price they sell it for. Our nation hasn't had a true leader since Ronald Reagan. Before than, we had Kennedy, before that, we had Lincoln, before that, we had Jackson, before that, we had Jefferson, and the very first and greatest President of all time was George Washington. Our nation lacks any and all leadership qualities. We give away everything and don't stay firm on almost any issues.

The Stance To Get Elected

To me, it looks like our country is being too generous with other nations and is giving everything to other countries in exchange for nothing. China can tax us whatever they want and our leaders will do nothing. Russia could opt out of a nuclear treaty and we would still remain in it by ourselves. Iran's leaders and citizens could chant "death to America" and our leaders might actually do something this time... give them about $100 Billion. It's disgraceful. Of course, all of these things actually happened, and the response of our leaders are 100% accurate.

The thing is that both Republicans and Democrats make the same mistake of idiocracy. If you identify with one of these parties, you may not be very much better than them, and if anything, you are helping them. It's called divide and conquer. If you had 100% resistance, you wouldn't succeed but if you had 50% resistance and 50% support, and some of the members of the resistance and supporters silence one another, you no longer have a full majority on either side. I am running as a Republican but I have Independent views. I would run as an Independent if it wouldn't bankrupt my political career. Sadly, in this day and age, it would.

While i'm on the subject of corrupt, evil, crooked, and horrible politicians and political systems, let me talk about the Federal Reserve. The Federal Reserve is one of the worst outputs from one of the worst administrations.

Woodrow Wilson was the most racist post civil war era presidents we have ever had. He also pulled a Bush and wrongfully got us into horrible wars that we had nothing to gain from at the cost of American taxpayers and thousands of lives.

Before I get back to the Federal reserve, let me just say, we're gonna end the draft. We will. As the great Ron Paul once stated, "If the war is worth fighting, people will volunteer".

You see, we're not sick like the rest of them. The rest of the politicians don't care what it costs, they will push their agenda at the expense of how ever many lives or how ever much cash it costs.

The Stance To Get Elected

The Federal Reserve was meant and created to put ourselves into a plethora of debt. The Federal Reserve isn't federal. In fact, it has shareholders, and they receive a 6% annual dividend. There also are 12 banks that own the Federal Reserve. Many of these banks are international banks. International banks have power over the United States money supply. Isn't that amazing? You can go to their website and you will see it.

Everytime we ask the Federal Reserve to print money, we go deeper into debt. That's right: the U.S. Government doesn't issue a penny. If we could, we would just issue enough to pay off our debts. We however can not do that. The Federal Reserve simply prints money out of nowhere. This paper is also worth absolutely nothing. Literally nothing. It's worth the paper it's printed on. It may have numbers printed on it but that means nothing if it's not backed by anything.

I am currently working on a replacement to the Federal Reserve, until then, we will audit the Federal Reserve. Later on during the campaign, I will release my replacement plan.

The Stance To Get Elected

Money is power, and debt is inevitable loss of that power. I don't know why other countries still let us borrow money from them. We owe $20 trillion. I'm going to end the National Debt. I will do it in 8 years if I am given the chance. I guarantee you. I will do this via a simple 3 point plan. Step one is ending all tax loopholes and abolishing some credits. Estimates say this will give about $200 Billion each year. Step two is to legalize and tax online gambling and marijuana, both at a 20% rate. Estimates show this will provide an extra $50 Billion each year. Finally, and most importantly, we will extract oil from the Green River Formation. There is about 2 Trillion barrels of extractable oil in this area. We will drill 5% of this each year, or about 100 Billion barrels each year. It will cost us about $2.5 Trillion each year to do this, but each year we will extract and sell $5 Trillion worth of oil, so we get $2.5 trillion each year. This plan will end our National Debt and create a small but still adequate surplus. After I end the National Debt, I will attempt to pass a bill or add an amendment that would force all future budgets to be equal to or less than the amount received that year in taxes. This would allow our nation to never again be in debt.

Wouldn't it be amazing if we were owed trillions and weren't forced into economic slavery? This is common sense people. No one else will say this. Republicans and Democrats alike won't say it because either they don't understand it, or they benefit from it. The elite benefit from anything, why wouldn't they benefit from this as well? I'm not saying they do, but I wouldn't throw it out.

I don't like to just talk about the bad, but you have to bring this stuff up to fix it. We lose a lot as a country. We win as well, but absolutely not as much as we should. Particularly, we lose at the immigration level. Other nation's aren't allowing refugees because they have seen what has happened to Europe. They have seen the horrors caused by some of them. I'm not saying all of them are bad, i'm not saying that at all. What I am saying is that some of them commit treacherous crimes, and set a precedent. The precedent is actually set in their country, but that's none of our business.

Anyways, Immigration is an amazing, and very encouraged thing. Our nation was founded on immigrants. These immigrants however didn't break any immigration laws when they came here. A lot of people nowadays do break laws we have in place in our country, and in exchange for breaking our laws, they ask and sometimes receive citizenship. Isn't that absurd? Now, with that being said, I kind of understand why they do it. People sit on the waiting list for 5 years to get into our country legally. Our current immigration system is horrible, in regards to speed at least. I will reform the system so that there is a que system implemented. I will allow people to come here legally quicker. There will be a maximum waiting period of 1 year for a response to your immigration application.

Let's say there are two people applying for citizenship, person A and person B. Person A is from a very safe and prosperous Dubai, and he applies for citizenship. He has a degree in college and has no criminal record. He however applied one year after person B applied, and person B does have a criminal record and is from a terror prone nation known as Iraq. Under my system, Person B would get priority over almost all. No longer will it be first come first serve. Admission into the greatest nation in the world will be exclusive to the people who have and will have the greatest potential in the world. No longer will we accept immigrants only to assist them through welfare for the rest of their life.

I also believe that we should innovate our border. The price of innovation will cost $1 Billion in taxpayer dollars, or about $10 per taxpayer. Although, we are going to create a surplus, so i'll reimburse you guys with 100% interest for it. If we implement the que system and increase funding by $1 Billion for deportations, drones/surveillance, and for border patrol agents, our border will be even more secure and Americans will be even more safe.

On the subject of money and taxpayer dollars, let me explain my tax plan. It's very simple. For the first three years, it will be a flat tax for all Americans of 20%. Nothing Less, nothing more. For corporations, it will be a 20% income tax with a 0.5% tax credit per 100,000 existing workers. Corporations will also have the opportunity to receive a tax credit of 1% for every 100,000 future employees they add. This will incentivize them to add hundreds of thousands of jobs. If they wanted to pay absolutely no income tax, they could employ 2.5 million workers, but we know that won't happen right? *laughter*. Oh, and I almost forgot, every fourth year of my administration, there will be no income tax. That's right, there will be a one year tax vacation every four years of my Presidency. Is that something you guys want? *Crowd exclaims yes*. Well, if you want that, vote for me, because I want that for you guys to. I also want that for our economy. Our economy will thrive under all years in my administration, but the economy will thrive most during the fourth year of my administration, and hopefully my eighth.

During my first year, I will add approximately 1.5 Million jobs, and during my first four years, I will add approximately 10 Million jobs. Next week I will be releasing a more detailed plan on how I plan on doing this.

The United States are the policemen of the world. We spend over $5 Billion every year on foreign aid, and for what in return? Our country shouldn't be willing to give away anything. Wwe should always try to win, and I will ensure that we will win. Even if it's just $1, we shouldn't give it away. We will cut foreign aid in half, as well as the cost. This will benefit ourselves, as well as the countries we are currently in. I however care more about our country than any other country, but there are still other humans that are being killed every day in those countries. Why don't we let the government of Syria deal with problems going on in Syria? We gain nothing if Syria becomes "Democratic" then elects another dictator in their first election after we spent $2 Trillion attempting to force democracy upon them. Our nation will prioritize America over all other countries. Of course we care about the refugees and all that but I care even more about the 50,000 homeless Veterans we have here in the U.S. I care more about the 15% of Americans that live below the poverty line. I care more about the millions of jobs being shipped overseas. I care more about the fact our economy is underperforming. I care more about the fact that U.S. companies have over $2.5 Trillion parked overseas. By the way, we're gonna get that cash that's parked overseas flowing into our country. We're gonna get it back. The reason companies don't bring their cash here is because we have insanely unfair tax rates. Companies don't want to give up over ⅓ of what they earned just because they are a corporation, and you wouldn't want to do that either. We are going to lower the rate in which that cash sitting overseas is taxed to 10%. We will offer a 10% reduction so the company pays absolutely no tax on the money brought overseas into the U.S. if they agree to put at least 20% of it into developing new facilities, adding new jobs, etc. Assuming all companies choose the 20% path, we will have a 3% GDP growth just from that alone. Also, when they decide to add new jobs, you will benefit. No longer will companies take jobs and cash overseas at no cost. You the people have been hurt too much by this. Our economy has been hurt by it aswell.

Election Day is a very sacred day, and it should be treated as such. We will make Election Day a National Holiday. This will ensure that everyone has the time to vote. We will also pass a law that makes sure there is at least 1 polling place per square mile. This will ensure everyone can vote as they will have the day off and will be less than one square mile away from a polling place.

However, if one would like to vote, they must have an ID. This isn't racist, and as a matter of fact, I will have withdrawn the power racists, as well as anyone else, have from halting anyone from voting by forcing there to be a polling place every square mile in the U.S. You need an ID to receive welfare, why don't you need one to decide the future of welfare? You also need an ID to buy some nail polish at CVS, buy some cold medicines, donate blood, to buy cigarettes, and many other things. Do you think nail polish is more important than the future of our nation? *crowd yells no* I don't think so either.

Our nation's water supply is being damaged. You can't drink the water in Flint, and you shouldn't drink the water from most of our public water supplies either. This is because it is pumped with fluoride. It has been estimated that over 40% of American children suffer from dental fluorosis. In case you didn't know, dental fluorosis is what happens when you have too much fluoride. The most common types of fluoride in our drinking water are sodium silicofluoride and hydrofluorosilicic acid. Both of these chemicals are unpurified waste products that are known to have higher levels of contaminants like arsenic. More than 23 human studies and more than 100 animal studies have linked fluoride to brain damage. Would you feed your child something that would give them brain damage? *crowd yells no* I wouldn't either. This is why we will end water fluoridation.

Also, the EPA has classified fluoride as a chemical with "substantial evidence of developmental neurotoxicity." It is also estimated that about 99% of the fluoride in our water gets put down the drain, and therefore pumped into the environment. This is not good. Doctor William Hirzy is a former EPA scientist. He states "If you want to prevent sunburn, you don't drink suntan lotion, you put it on your skin. If you want to have the benefits of fluoride and oral health … you put it on the surface of the tooth. You don't drink it." Water fluoridation is the first and only drug forced to the masses as forced medication with no control over dosage. This is also the last of those forced medications.

Space exploration and advancements in science are very very important to me. I feel like our civilization is not growing at the rate we could be. I want my administration to be known as "The Era Of Advancements". I will multiply

NASA's budget by 5, improve the FDA, and we as a nation will advance scientifically significantly. I would love for my administration to no longer make it normal to be diagnosed with cancer in America. I want to end cancer. Eliminate it from the face of the Earth. Someone has to do it at some point. I would like for we as a nation to explore space. Manned exploration or not, I would like to do it. I would like to find alien life. That would be amazing. I absolutely believe it exists. There is no way we are alone. It is basically impossible that we are alone.

If there is evidence that I am given that shows there is extraterrestrial life out there, you better believe it will be released. I am not sure if the President is given this information or if this information exists but as I said if it does, you will know about it. I will lead of by and for the people, just like Abraham Lincoln. Any information available to me that would prove or disprove any "conspiracy theory" will be released to the public. This goes for all conspiracy theories, I don't want any Americans to feel insecure about the government. I want to fix the government because right now even I feel insecure about it.

We as a country have astronomically high drug prices. You guys are hurt from this since this means that you must pay much more for your medication than you should. We are going to open the hell out of our markets, wide open. Let the medication flow into our market, and let the prices fall.

I hate big tobacco, and i'm pretty sure the feeling is mutual. I want to eradicate big tobacco from the face of the earth, as well as eliminate the deaths associated with second hand smoke. Tens of thousands die every year because some idiot decided they wanted to pump chemicals into their lungs and exhale those chemicals into the air everyone must breathe. Most of the people that die because of the idiots are children. It's so sad. But you know what? Big tobacco doesn't care. They only care about profit. Big tobacco would rather have those children become addicted to cigarettes as well, and as long as they buy some cigarettes, they don't care if they die. We're going to make it illegal to smoke in public and we are going to raise the federal tax rate on cigarettes to $10. This will make sure that people don't even think about smoking. All of the federal tax revenue that comes from the cigarette tax will go towards ads that are anti-cigarette, help towards current smokers, and the rebuilding of communities crushed by big tobacco. Typically these communities are in poverty, so big tobacco targets them. It's so sad. It'll stop though... it'll stop.

We as a nation are divided. We have been since we were founded, but it has been getting worse lately. But you see, this is one of the beautiful things in America. I don't like division but I do like the right to have varying opinions. However, on some issues, it is just common sense. My campaign will be the common sense campaign. I will solve issues in a way that benefits the nation, no matter who is happy in the end. I would like to make everyone happy but there is always going to be an opposition to something. You can never please 100% of the people. But you know what you can do? You can do what is right for America, no matter what the pollsters say. What is right is what is right and what is wrong is what is wrong. Nothing less and nothing more. I will attempt to ensure that we are not a nation divided but in the end, I care more about the nation than I do my approval rating. I do love you guys though. Aren't you guys the best? *crowd cheers*

One topic we tend not to be divided on is education. Education is key to a successful society, and sadly our public educational system isn't doing too good compared to other nations. We are ranked 14th in education globally. Should America ever be in 14th place? *crowd yells no* I don't think so either. If we are to fix the plethora of errors in our educational system, there must be a plan... so here it is. Our public education system is from the 18th century when the vast majority of Americans were farmers and schools didn't have air conditioning. Our system shouldn't just be K-12 with long Summer breaks in the middle of all of it. A Harvard study found that if children don't receive early brain stimulation, they will not thrive in the future academically. We will make pre-school mandatory across the nation. This will help children get the early learning boost that they desperately need. To pay for this whole system, we will cut out the 12th grade. This will boost high school graduation rates, college enrollment, and employment rates and will overall benefit our country. We also will create a 4-3 educational system where you have four days of school then three days off. The amount of days kids get off of school where vary locally but we will require 210 days of mandatory instruction. This new schedule will help improve America as a whole.

We will also end property tax based education. Most states rely on property taxes to fund the educational system, but since wealthy houses are worth more so they pay more in taxes, the wealthy zip codes get better schools and therefore a better education than most. It will be up to the states to determine the amount but the amount of money taken from property taxes and put into the education system will need to be even or flat. No longer will the rich get to go to the good schools and the poor get to go to the bad schools. All schools will be good in America, it is called American exceptionalism, and our education system will be no different from the rest of America in the fact that we will be the best and excel at everything that we do! *crowd cheers*

Now it's time to tackle an area with opposition: healthcare. There are many different ideas as to how healthcare should work in America, but this idea is the most beneficial idea, at least towards the country as a whole. A person with common sense but an evil personality would say that the solution to the outrageous premium prices would be to cut sick people off of health insurance so that way only healthy people have health insurance and they don't use it, so therefore premiums will go down. This solution however doesn't work.

I want costs to go down and I don't want people to be dying in the streets. Prevention is key to this. When people notice they have a "bug" or a mere amount of back pain, they must consult help and if they don't let the illness snowball, costs for them or the insurance company will be drastically less. We must encourage early extermination of illnesses and support new medications that entirely eradicate certain diseases from America. That isn't entirely my healthcare plan but it would help bring down costs if it occurred.

If we are to fix the healthcare system, we must allow individuals and employers to opt out of the individual mandate. The employer mandate makes all companies or firms with 50 or more employees to pay for insurance for the employees. Almost 100% of people support the repeal of this as it is economically detrimental. It has caused a huge reduction in full time employment. This is bad. What is even worse is that some estimates state that that when the act is fully implemented, tens of millions of people could lose their health insurance that is sponsored by their employers. We will repeal the mandate, something most people would support, and by doing so, we will shrink the amount of money we take out of American's paychecks by about $282 Billion over the next 10 years.

I do not like the mandates we have in place, and neither does the economy. I will repeal the mandate implemented on seniors regarding Medicare. Seniors should be able to also opt out of this mandate. You kind of can opt out of Medicare right now but doing so would result in the loss of your Social Security benefits. To the average person, the people who truly are America, this is impossible to do. RIght now, ⅓ of doctors refuse to take Medicaid patients. This is due to government reimbursements. What do you think is going to happen to the Medicare patients when Medicare's rates become worse than Medicaid? I'll tell you what will happen, according to the Medicare agency, about 15% of the hospitals in America will go out of business. When something causes 15% of a sector to go out of business, that thing is very bad. If Seniors had the opportunity to opt out of Medicare, alternative solutions in private insurance companies would appear. It may not be the best at first because actually, Medicare is good economically for most American families but over time, it would work out as more and more Seniors would leave Medicare as the effects that have compounded continue to snowball and it would be overall better for Seniors. Freedom is a right given to all Americans, ALL. Freedom shouldn't just be given to those under 65, all Americans should have freedom to choose their healthcare, and in the end it is a choice.

I also am a very strong supporter of HSAs, or Health Savings Accounts. We had 50 million uninsured prior to the implementation of Obamacare and will still have 30 million uninsured after the full implementation of Obamacare. This may look good at the surface but simply making more people have more insurance in this country doesn't help. As a matter of fact, it makes it worse. Anyways, the reason we had and still will have so many people uninsured is because healthcare is extremely expensive. Obamacare has done nothing to combat this problem and has done lots to make this problem worse, at times up to 67% worse. Many different experts have come up with different solutions to the mess regarding our healthcare system but all of the solutions trace back to HSAs.

HSAs help bring the cost of healthcare down by putting individuals in charge of their healthcare. When you have to pay for your own healthcare, you will question all tests and costs that are proposed to you. Doctors and hospitals will then need to be more responsive to your needs or they will lose your business. Also, the price of certain tests will need to be affordable or no one will get them. This will help lower costs and make healthcare overall more affordable. But that's not it. Everyone will be able to use after-tax dollars to pay for HSAs. Health Savings Accounts already exist but a mere 5% of Americans use them. If every American had HSAs, the cost of healthcare would definitely go down. We are going to just this by changing the law. Currently not everyone is eligible to have an HSA. We will make it so everyone can have one. We will make it illegal to not have an HSA. You don't have to use your HSA as your primary source of healthcare, but you would be stupid not to. This is since we will make it great. We will remove all caps on the amount you can put into them, as well as your employer. We will make it so your employer must put in a certain of your salary into an HSA, and you can use it for whatever you want in regards to your medical needs. For those who make $10,000 or less per year, employers must pay 10% of the salary. For those who make $10,001 to $25,000, employers must pay 4% of the salary. For those who make $25,001 to $50,000, employers must pay 2% of the salary. For those who make $50,001 to $100,000, employers must pay 1% of their salary. For those who make more than $100,000 annually, employers must put in 0% and the worker must put in an amount they choose, they must however put some money into an HSA. This will make everyone have an HSA and the vast majority of people having one without needing to put money into it. If they do however put more money into it, they will be able to do so tax free and at the amount they choose, rather than paying a monthly payment on health insurance that most rarely use to pay for very expensive items, you can have an HSA and spend however much you want on whatever expenses you want. It's all your choice.

This plan may make me seem like I am anti business. This absolutely is not the case. I want businesses to grow. Small businesses are the foundation of our country. This is why we will encourage small business growth and development. We will do this by removing the very discouraging regulations and extremely high taxes that businesses must pay. The corporate tax rate will be lowered to 20%. We also will get the trillions that are sitting offshore back into our country, as I stated earlier. We will do this by taxing them at a 10% rate or a 0% rate, depending on what they choose to do. Small businesses will no longer be taxed out of business with the new corporate tax rate. I'll release more soon on policies I will enact that will create more jobs in my two terms than any other President in history and create more GDP growth than any other President.

Social security is horrible for everyone. Social security secures nothing but a poor life for seniors and debt for future generations. Not a good combo. A simple solution to social security is the total abolition of this system. This is basically what I will do. All Americans who have put money into social security will need to do the same for the rest of their lives, and all who currently receive benefits will get those benefits. All Americans who have not put any money into social security will not have to.

You might be asking why I want to do this. Well, the answer lies in debt, the fact we don't need the system, and government inefficiency. The U.S. Treasury owes $2.8 Trillion to the Social Security Trust Fund. To put it simply, we are spending more money than we take in while giving out guaranteed benefits that barely put retirees above the poverty line. 25% of the U.S. budget is dedicated to Social Security every year, or about $900 Billion. This is a large sum of money that is spent to keep Americans just $5,000 over the poverty level. Also, 33.3% of Americans have no other retirement savings, so the only benefits they receive will be social security benefits that will barely be enough to keep them above the poverty level. This however is the current benefits. Estimates state that by 2034, there will be a 21% reduction to social security benefits. This will make retirees just $1,000 over the poverty level.

There however is a solution. If we made it law that all employed people at age 18 and above must put at least 3.7% of their salary into a retirement savings account of their choice, the situation for them and the government would be much better. The government will no longer offer Social Security benefits when the last person that put money into social security dies and therefore will no longer need to spend Billions each year on the failed system and go Trillions deeper into debt. Anyways, the 3.7% is far less than the government gets, they get 6.2% out of your paycheck and another 6.2% from your employer. This is 12.4% of your income. The maximum amount of money this 12.4% tax can get you annually when you retire is $31,668 each year, and remember, this number will go down as time progresses. The numbers would be a lot worse for Social Security if the numbers were the same. Assume you made the average salary in America of about $33,200. If you made that money and started putting money into social security at age 18, when you retired at age 67, you would get about $13,000 per year in pensions. This is with no inflation or salary increases. Now, let's assume the you made the same amount of money but instead of putting money into social security, you put 3.7% of your $33,200 you made each year into a retirement savings account. Well, if this happened, the amount of money you saved would allow you to make about $32,500 each year, until you turned 82. This is 250% of what you got with social security, except it's ⅓ of the price. By the way, the life expectancy in America is 79, so you would be living longer than average in this scenario and still make more than you would with social security. Even if you lived until 100, something 0.02% of Americans do, you would make about $20,600 per year, 158% of what you would get with social security.

This solution is so much better and allows you to make 2.5% more every year. It's a win win win. It's a win for you as you make more when you retire and while you are working. It's a win for the government as they no longer must deal with the Trillions of dollars in debt associated with the program. Finally, It's a win for companies as they no longer must pay a large sum of money into a failed system, and now they get to put that money into the economy. Overall, we are going to do something nobody else can do properly: fix social security. The differences in our plan and the plans of everyone else is that our plan doesn't just stall the time in which social security will fail, it stops social security from failing and helps everyone out far more than any other plan would.

There will be many different arguments as to what causes climate change but it is a fact that it is occurring. I personally believe that climate change is occurring and there are things we could do to make the situation better, but it's not entirely our fault. However, for the simple fact that climate change is occurring, our nation will "go green", kind of. We don't want to regulate businesses out of business. We will not set any regulations but will trust corporations, yes i know, we shouldn't trust the corporations but hear me out, trust the corporations and see if they can hit the goal we have set: a 1% drop in CO_2 emissions. I would like for us to continue to have 1% drops every year throughout my administration. The corporations can do whatever they want to make this happen, it will be totally up to them. I believe the corporations will fulfil the goals we have set forth and if they don't, something will happen. But you guys have to realize that even CO_2 emissions aren't entirely our fault. Yes, there are things humans do that cause CO_2 emissions but some of the emissions do occur naturally. Also, the benefits of the number one contributor to CO_2 emissions, the burning of fossil fuels, far outweigh the bad. Fossil fuels are a cheap and plentiful reliable energy source that helps make modern life possible and compared to the efficiency of other energy sources, none can match. Do you like your life? *crowd yells yes* I do too. I would also like to debunk the "97% of scientists" claim. Firstly, science is not democratic. It used to be the consensus that the Earth was flat but then all it took was one individual to say that it wasn't and we soon realized it wasn't, so even if the figure was true, it means nothing really. Secondly, if 97% of scientists believe humans are the cause of it, it has to come from somewhere. I won't go into detail about where the number originated from, it is an outdated number created falsely. Instead, since so many continue to cite the figure today, I would like to ask anyone who disagrees with me to gather the names of every scientist in the world and then get his or her stance on climate change and what the primary cause is. I guarantee you the number will not be 97%. Polls are very inaccurate, including the one's continuously cited today that claim 97% of scientists believe human cause is the primary cause of climate change. As I stated before, climate change is occurring, and there are things humans can do that would help reverse the effects, but it isn't entirely our fault. I still however will lower CO_2 emissions and try to help in the ways I can that benefit everyone, and we'll see what happens.

Ever since 9/11, national security has been a very popular topic of political discussion. I will make sure that terrorism doesn't reach the United States. I will also take the huge target off of our back by removing troops from all around the world. As sad as it is if a foreigner is hurt or killed by another foreigner, we must first worry about non-foreigners. These people are known as Americans and they matter the most to me. I care more about my country than I do about the world. I would choose Americanism over Globalism every single day, and if I am elected President, I will make sure America's prosperity is the number one priority.

Anyways, my National Security plan involves growing the U.S. military.

This however doesn't have to be done through more military spending. Like I said earlier, how is it possible for other countries to grow militaristically at a faster rate than us yet spend ⅓ of what we spend? I will grow the military at no extra cost. National security nowadays is also dependent on cyber security. I will improve our country's cyber defense and ensure our grid and other cyber firms aren't vulnerable to potential attacks from the enemy. One way we also will help our country is through the foundation of the URC. The URC will be an agreement/treaty with the United States, China, and Russia, the three superpowers of the world. The URC will be a militaristic treaty only and would expire after 10 years, with the possibility of renewal. This agreement would help the U.S. as we could destroy terrorism threats much easier. I go into more detail in my URC Plan that I will release next week. Overall, under my presidency, the United States will remain a superpower of the world and will be a safe nation for its citizens.

Before I leave the subject of National Security, let me say that privacy and national security can both be achieved. We are going to repeal the Patriot Act that is one of the most unpatriotic acts passed in the history of our nation. We will not take away basic human rights at the expense of stopping potential terrorists. We will come up with better ways to ensure we are safe. There are two different strategies that could keep us safe: peace through strength, what has kept us pretty much unharmed throughout the last 50 years, or what I call simple peace. Simple peace is the elimination of nuclear weapons and the implementation of more diplomatic ways to tackle situations. I believe a mixture of these are key to safety. The effects of nuclear weapons are bad, and the leaders of countries that have nukes know this. This is why they have only been used twice in human history. Arguments can be made that would say that nukes are good because of this but overall, I would like to eliminate the risk. I would support the destruction of all of our nukes, only if other countries were willing to do the same thing. I would rather avoid a fight but if a fight is to occur, I would like to fight back. I want our military to be so strong we don't have to use it rather than so weak that we can not use it. Ending nuclear capabilities of all counties would be good for humanity as a whole. What is stopping one madman over in North Korea from starting WW3 by pushing the button? When given the choice, I would rather have some damage be caused and some brave soldiers die in warfare than have humans go extinct, but I would rather avoid both scenarios and have us go back to the issues that matter.

Congress has and always will be vastly unpopular. This is because they are unable to properly function due to "party lines". Some things that are more popular than Congress are root canals, lice, traffic jams, and cockroaches * crowd laughs*. I will destroy the party lines and encourage Congress to vote on what is truly good, not what their party leaders say to vote on. I want to work with Congress, no matter who controls the majority, to help America seek something better. That is exactly what we will do ladies and gentlemen: seek something better. We will do this if I am elected President. So, everyone, I have officially begun one hell of a journey that will be spent fighting for all of us. I am running for President of the

United States. Thank you- Thank you very much *cheers*

This speech would resonate well with most and would be one of the first times I will be given mainstream media attention. It will work out for me and my campaign.

Chapter Three
Staff And Advisors

"Surround yourself with people who will lift you higher." -Oprah Winfrey

---

It is essential to have good advisors and staff if I am to have a good campaign. I will have 10 great members of my staff that will help America seek something better.

My campaign manager will be someone who has political experience, is scandal free, leans to the right, will not try to run the show, and will be good at raising funds from the people, not special interest groups or super pacs. My campaign manager would be someone like a Rand Paul. My campaign manager would be instructed to raise $500 million solely from the people in the primaries and $1 billion solely from the people in the general election. They also would be instructed to represent me and schedule as many media appearances as possible. Free publicity is the best publicity, whether negative or positive. I would pay my campaign manager a salary of $250,000.

I will also have a chief strategist on my team. I would want them to play mind games with everyone. I would want them to have a step by step plan for everything, say one thing to make someone else say another, etc. They also must be very experienced, but I would prefer them to be an outsider. They could have past experiences in law or in politics in general. I don't care, as long as I trust them and they have a good vision and the determination to go through with that vision, they will be hired. My chief strategist would be someone like an Andrew Jackson or a Trey Gowdy. My chief strategist would get a salary of $200,000 per year.

Thirdly, I will have a political director as a member of the campaign. They will basically be in charge of the campaign decisions and will essentially create the agenda for the campaign. It will be a very important position. This position will be filled by someone who has known me. It will be filled by my past communications director when I got elected to the House of Representatives. The salary for this position will be $175,000.

Also, I will have a communications director on my staff. They will be the main spokesperson of the campaign. They will basically be the ambassador of the Bono campaign. This role will be key to helping us get elected. I would like to simply hire a communications strategist I believe in. I'm not sure who it will be but it will be someone with the mindset of a businessman, possibly a CEO. I like people with a business mindset, they get things done. I want this to be the same for my communications director. Whoever fills this position will get a salary of $150,000.

The fifth position I will have on my staff is social media director. They will need to master something that is key to mastering engagement: social media. If you use it right, you can attract millions of people simply by using 140 characters or posting a picture or phrase. I need help getting engagement up online. I would like every event I have to be live streamed on Facebook and Instagram to attract people to my page. I need an experienced person to help me do this. I would like to hire someone with a social media base themselves that they could bring to me, and then manage. Again, i'm not sure who will fill this position but I would like for it to be someone like Ann Coulter. Whoever fills this position will be paid a $125,000 salary.

The sixth position that will be filled will be my informal advisor. I want my informal advisor to tell me the other side of things. I need him to be what the media might call a "conspiracy theorist". I can tell when things are true or not, I would just like to hear both sides of a story instead of surrounding myself with the same types of people. My informal advisor will basically tell me what he knows or believes in and why. I will then make an opinion on that based on lots of information. I would like this position to be filled by someone like a Matt Drudge or maybe even an Alex Jones. It also very easily could be someone else who fits my criteria. Whoever it ends up being, they will make a salary of $150,000.

The next position that must be filled in my staff is my senior advisor. My senior advisor will be a more trusted source of info so I along with my staff don't get too heavily criticized. It will be someone like a Marco Rubio or a Bernie Sanders. My senior advisor will simply advise me on issues. They will get paid $150,000.

The eighth position on my staff will be my policy director. My policy director will do the obvious: help solve policy issues. They will help me out on policy issues. The position will be filled by someone that simply has beliefs that coincide with my own, like a Rand Paul or a Ted Cruz or a Donald Trump. The senior advisor will get a salary of $125,000.

The ninth position in my staff will be my national security/foreign policy advisor. They will advise me on all issues in relation to national security or foreign policy. I would like this person to have military experience but not be a warmonger. We'll see who this person ends up being. They will earn a $175,000 salary.

The final position on my staff will be my delegate strategist. My delegate strategist will help draw paths for me to get the Republican nomination. This will help me know where to campaign. They then will help me in the general election by making paths to 270 electoral votes. I would like this position to be given to someone who has had past election experience. I want this position to be filled by someone like John Kasich. My delegate strategist will receive a salary of $125,000.

Overall, I will have a great staff that will work effortlessly with me to help us seek something better, and they will have key roles in making me the President of the United States in 2040.

Chapter Four
The Media

"Whoever controls the media, controls the mind." -Jim Morrison

---

The media is essential to winning an election. You need coverage. You need your name to get out there. You need people to see your message. You must manipulate the media.

The first part of my plan involves getting immediate coverage in the beginning of the campaign. I don't care if the coverage is good or bad, as long as I am covered. I want my name to stick in the media for a long time. This will probably be done do to statements I made or will make. I also will invite the media to all of my "big announcements" that will really just be campaign rallies. The rallies will be small at first but media coverage will make them larger.

Step two of my plan is to get the media to interview me. Offer "exclusive" interviews. This will only be done during the first 1-2 months of my campaign. This will once again help my message get to people and it will seem as though I am being transparent. I also will get my message out via ads. Ads will be talked about more in depth later on but my ad campaign will be amazing.

Step three of my media plan is to turn on the media. I will criticize them, as everyone should be criticized. No one in this world is exempt from criticism. The media will then begin to cover me more negatively, and more often, which will benefit me.

Step four is to turn the public against the media, even more than they are right now. According to Gallup, a mere 32% of people trust the mainstream media. That number should be lower, and i'll make sure that it will be. My huge amount of supporters will all be turned against the media because of me. It won't be violent, they simply won't trust or follow the mainstream media. I myself have, to an extent, amounts of respect or trust in the media but it is better for my campaign if the media is manipulated. Also, the small amount of trust I do have in the mainstream media could disappear overnight if they continue to report or act the way that they do. MSNBC for example is a total joke. CNN is bad and biased but still slightly ok, FOX is biased, NBC and

ABC just follow CNN, and BBC is probably the best in terms of accurate and fair reporting.

Step five is to expose the media. 6 companies control 90% of the media in America. These 6 companies are General Electric, News-Corp, Disney, Viacom, Time Warner, and CBS. No wonder you are fed the same information from practically every channel you go to. 232 media executives control the information that is given to over 277 million Americans. This is means each media executive controls what about 1.2 million people see. The revenue in 2010 of these 6 companies was about $280 billion. This was $40 billion more than the GDP of Finland, or enough to buy every NFL team 12 times, and still have money leftover. 178 million different users read Time Warner's news each month. The News-Corp company owns the top newspaper in 3 continents. In 2010, News-Corp avoided $1 billion in taxes. This is enough to double the budget of FEMA or to fund NPR 40 times. Box office sales of the 6 companies was $7 billion in 2010. This is double the sales of the next 140 studios combined. It's sad... back in 1983, 90% of the media was controlled by 50 companies. Overall, there are 1,500 magazines, 1,100 newspapers, 9,000 radio stations, 1,500 TV stations, and 2,400 publishers run by these 6 companies. If more people knew this, the approval rating of the mainstream media would surely drop. The media would surely fight this, even though you can't fight facts, and I would get even more coverage.

Step six is to funnel mainstream media viewers over to my social media page. Like I said earlier, every single event I have will be livestreamed and posted onto my social media pages. I also will make lots of announcements on my social media page, forcing people to follow me, including the media, if they would like to hear what I have to say, and they will definitely want to hear what I have to say as at this point I will have formed large group of supporters and will be the favorite to win the nomination. People will watch my speeches on social media rather than the media.

Finally, step seven will be to maintain the position I will be in. I will have won my war with the media and annihilated their credibility. I will have a huge following on social media and anyone who still watches the mainstream media will still watch constant coverage of me.

Chapter Five
Funding

"It always seems impossible until it's done"
-Nelson Mandela

I will spend more than any other candidate in history on my campaign. I will get $500 million by the convention and will get another $1 billion through the general election season. Overall, I will spend $1.5 billion on my campaign. Here's the breakdown of my sources of revenue during the campaign.

PRIMARIES

Type Of Donor	Percentage Of Revenue
Individual	80%
Super Pacs	<1%
RNC	13%
Other	6%

The vast majority of funding will come from individuals and practically no funding will come from super PACs.

GENERAL ELECTION

Type Of Donor	Percentage Of Revenue
Individuals	81%
Super Pacs	1%
RNC	17%
Other	1%

Again, the vast majority of my funding will come from individuals in the general election. 98% of my revenue comes from the RNC and individual donations.

I will spend 100% of what I receive and overall will run a good successful campaign.

Chapter Six
The Primary Rallies

"Government is not the solution to the problem; government is the problem." -Ronald Reagan

---

My first rally will be in May of 2039. It will be in whatever state the first primary will be in. I will have a town hall there later that week as well. I will have basically one political rally per day, sometimes two or three. I will put a possible schedule below with the location and the estimated size of the crowd. I would like to hold a rally with 50,000 people in attendance in each state throughout the primary season.

Possible Schedule
- May 2- State where first primary is, 5,000 in crowd
- May 3- Pennsylvania, Wells Fargo Center, 20,000 in crowd
- May 4- North Carolina, Cameron Indoor Stadium, 9,000 in crowd
- May 5- South Carolina, Bon Secours Wellness Arena, 12,000 in crowd
- May 6- Atlanta, Georgia, Phillips Arena, 20,000 in crowd

- May 7- State where first primary is, first town hall, 7,500 in crowd
- May 8- Utah, Vivint Smart Home Arena, 20,000 in crowd
- May 9- Nevada, T-Mobile Arena, 15,000 in crowd
- May 10- Arizona, Scottsdale Stadium, 10,000 in crowd
- May 11- Michigan, The Palace of Auburn Hills, 20,000 in crowd
- May 12- State where first primary is, 10,000 in crowd
- May 13- Missouri, Scottrade Center, 17,500 in crowd
- May 14- Pennsylvania, Beaver Stadium, 50,000+ in crowd
- June 5- Texas, Globe Life Park, 50,000+ in crowd
- June 10- North Dakota, Alerus Center, 50,000+ in crowd
- June 11- New Hampshire, SNHU Arena, 10,000 in crowd
- June 12- Maine, Alfond Arena, 10,000 in crowd
- June 17- Kentucky, Commonwealth Stadium, 50,000+ in crowd
- June 19- Oregon, Moda Center, 20,000 in crowd

- June 25- Colorado, Broadmoor World Arena, 10,000 in crowd
- July 1- Florida, FIU Stadium, 20,000 in crowd
- July 2- Alaska, Sullivan Arena, 10,000 in crowd
- July 3- Illinois, Toyota Park, 25,000 in crowd
- July 4- Louisiana, Independence Stadium, 50,000+ in crowd
- July 16- Connecticut, Yale Bowl, 50,000+ in crowd
- July 24- Virginia, Bridgeforth Stadium, 25,000 in crowd
- July 30- Ohio, Quicken Loans Arena, 20,000 in crowd
- August 5- Indiana, Memorial Stadium, 50,000+ in crowd
- August 7- Tennessee, Liberty Bowl Memorial Stadium, 50,000+ in crowd
- August 16- West Virginia, WVU Coliseum, 15,000 in crowd
- August 19- Kansas, Allen Fieldhouse, 17,500 in crowd
- August 24- New Mexico, The Pit, 15,000 in crowd
- August 26- Oklahoma, Boone Pickens Stadium, 50,000+ in crowd

- August 27- Iowa, UNI Dome, 17,500 in crowd
- August 28- Idaho, Albertsons Stadium, 50,000+ in crowd
- September 9- Arkansas, War Memorial Stadium, 50,000+ in crowd
- September 11- New York, Yankee Stadium, 50,000+ in crowd
- September 17- Wisconsin, Miller Park, 50,000+ in crowd
- September 24- Minnesota, Mariucci Arena, 10,000 in crowd
- September 30- Florida, Bright House Networks Stadium, 50,000+ in crowd
- October 2-Alabama, Ladd=Peebles Stadium, 50,000+ in crowd
- October 7- Mississippi, M. M. Roberts Stadium, 50,000+ in crowd
- October 8- Hawaii, Aloha Stadium, 50,000+ in crowd
- October 9- Massachussetts, Fitton Field, 25,000 in crowd
- October 12- New Jersey, High Point Solutions Stadium, 50,000+ in crowd
- October 14- Rhode Island, Brown Stadium, 50,000+ in crowd
- October 16- Nebraska, TD Ameritrade Park Omaha, 50,000+ in crowd

The Stance To Get Elected

- October 18- South Dakota, Dana J. Dykhouse Stadium, 50,000+ in crowd
- October 20- California, Staples Center, 20,000 in crowd
- October 21- California, Angel Stadium of Anaheim, 50,000+ in crowd
- October 23- Washington, Joe Albi Stadium, 25,000 in crowd
- October 25- Oregon, Reser Stadium, 50,000+ in crowd
- October 28- Vermont, Centennial Field, 25,000 in crowd
- October 29- Maryland, Navy Marine Corps Memorial Stadium, 50,000+ in crowd
- October 30- Delaware, Delaware Stadium, 50,000+ in crowd
- November 1- Ewing M. Kauffman Stadium, 50,000+ in crowd
- November 4- Montana, Metrapark Arena, 15,000 in crowd
- November 5- Wyoming, Arena Auditorium, 20,000 in crowd
- November 6- Colorado, Coors Field, 50,000+ in crowd
- November 10- Arizona, Chase Field, 50,000+ in crowd

- November 12- Kansas, University of Kansas Memorial Stadium, 50,000+ in crowd
- November 14- Ohio, InfoCision Stadium, 50,000+ in crowd
- November 15- Montana, Washington-Grizzly Stadium, 50,000+ in crowd
- November 18- Virginia, EagleBank Arena, 15,000 in crowd
- November 19- North Carolina, PNC Arena, 25,000 in crowd
- November 20- Pennsylvania, PNC Park, 30,000 in crowd
- November 25- Texas, Gerald J. Ford Stadium, 50,000+ in crowd
- November 27- South Carolina, Williams-Brice Stadium, 50,000+ in crowd
- November 29- Iowa, Jack Trice Stadium, 50,000+ in crowd
- December 4- state where first primary is, 20,000 in crowd
- December 10- New Mexico, University Stadium, 50,000+ in crowd
- December 11- Georgia, Turner Field, 50,000+ in crowd

- December 16- Massachussetts, Harvard Stadium, 25,000 in crowd
- December 21- Michigan, Waldo Stadium, 30,000 in crowd
- December 30- Alaska, Anchorage Football Field, 25,000 in crowd
- December 31- Pennsylvania, Hershey Park Arena, 10,000 in crowd
- January 1- California, Honda Center, 17,500 in crowd
- January 5- Utah, Rice Eccles Stadium, 50,000+ in crowd
- January 6- Indiana, Banker's Life Fieldhouse, 15,000 in crowd
- January 10- Michigan, Comerica Park, 50,000+ in crowd
- January 13- Minnesota, Target Field, 50,000+ in crowd
- January 15- Maine, Cross Insurance Arena, 10,000 in crowd
- January 20- Nevada, Sam Boyd Stadium, 50,000+ in crowd
- January 22- New Hampshire, Wildcat Stadium, 25,000 in crowd
- January 28- Illinois, Huskie Stadium, 50,000+ in crowd
- February 3- Massachusetts, Fenway Park, 50,000+ in crowd

The Stance To Get Elected

- February 5- Florida, Lockhart Stadium, 20,000 in crowd
- February 7- Virginia, John C. Edwards Stadium, 50,000+ in crowd
- February 11- Wisconsin, Kohl Center, 20,000 in crowd
- February 17- North Carolina, Ficklen Stadium, 50,000+ in crowd
- February 21- Iowa, Wells Fargo Arena, 15,000 in crowd
- February 25- Oregon, Matthew Knight Arena, 12,500 in crowd
- February 26- New Hampshire, International Speedway, 50,000+ in crowd
- March 2- North Carolina, Cameron Indoor Stadium, 10,000 in crowd
- March 4- New Mexico, Isotopes Park, 15,000 in crowd
- March 7- Oregon, Hayward Field, 12,500 in crowd
- March 11- Florida- Amalie Arena, 15,000 in crowd
- March 17- Wyoming, War Memorial Stadium, 50,000+ in crowd
- March 18- Virginia, John Paul Jones Arena, 15,000 in crowd

- March 21- California, Titian Stadium, 12,500 in crowd
- March 23- Pennsylvania, Howard J. Lamade Stadium, 45,000 in crowd
- March 24- Florida, Blue Wahoos Stadium, 10,000 in crowd
- March 25- Ohio, Nationwide Arena, 12,500 in crowd
- March 30- Michigan, Crisler Center, 12,500 in crowd
- April 5- Iowa, Buccaneer Arena, 5,000 in crowd
- April 6- Arizona, Surprise Stadium, 10,000 in crowd
- April 8- Nevada, Reno EVents Center, 7,500 in crowd
- April 10- New Hampshire, Holman Stadium, 7,500
- April 14- Alaska, The Dome, 50,000+ in crowd
- April 20- Florida, BB&T Center, 12,500 in crowd
- April 22- Colorado, 1stBank Center, 7,500 in crowd
- April 28- Pennsylvania, Giant Center, 10,000 in crowd
- May 3- Florida, American Airlines Arena, 20,000 in crowd

- May 5- New Hampshire, SNHU Arena, 12,500 in crowd
- May 9- Minnesota, Williams Arena, 12,500 in crowd
- May 11- Wisconsin, BMO Harris Bradley Center, 15,000 in crowd
- May 12- Ohio, Huntington Center, 7,500 in crowd
- May 13- Arizona, University Of Phoenix Stadium, 25,000 in crowd
- May 14- New Mexico, Roswell Convention Center, 2,500 in crowd
- May 16- California, Redding Civic Auditorium, 2,500 in crowd
- May 17- Oregon, Providence Park, 15,000 in crowd
- May 19- Connecticut, XL Center, 15,000 in crowd
- May 22- New Jersey, Red Bull Arena, 20,000 in crowd
- May 25- Maine, Alfond Stadium, 50,000+ in crowd
- May 26- Rhode Island, Dunkin Donuts Center, 10,000 in crowd
- May 31- Pennsylvania, Beaver Stadium, 75,000+ in crowd

Chapter Seven
The First Debate

"Without debate, without criticism, no administration and no country can succeed-- and no republic can survive." -John F. Kennedy

---

The first Republican debate should be sometime between May and August of 2039. Going into the debate, I intend to be in the top 3 in terms of polling. The debate will be a great opportunity for me to get my name and policies out there without having to pay a premium for ads. There will also be far more viewers of the debate than almost any ad could attract. I will spend about 70% of my speaking time talking about my policies and 30% of my speaking time attacking other candidates and their policies or history. My attacks will be very effective. I am going to get as much attention as is possible during this debate.

Overall, the first debate will be a very good experience and will help my numbers spike. My crowd sizes will grow after the first debate and step three of my media plan will commence at my first rally after the debate after I get good coverage and reviews from the media.

The Stance To Get Elected

Chapter Eight
The First
Primary/Caucus

"There's no such thing as a free lunch."
-Milton Friedman

I probably will lose the first primary or caucus. I was a one term governor of Pennsylvania and member of the House of Representatives. I wasn't even a Senator. This however doesn't mean that I won't win the nomination or won't get any delegates from the first primary or caucus.

I expect there to be 10 candidates in the race at this point. I then expect to place in third in the first primary with about 24% of the vote. I will get some delegates for this as well. Following defeat in the first primary, with nothing else to lose, I will have delegates to gain. I will drastically improve my ground game and will have my delegate strategist give me five separate scenarios in which I win certain states that will win me the nomination. I will then go through with the plans and win far more delegates and eventually the nomination.

Chapter Nine
Future
Primaries/Caucuses

"To be prepared for war is one of the most effectual means of preserving peace."

After my defeat in the first primary or caucus, I will win every single primary or caucus after that until "Super Tuesday" comes. I will win the majority of the states on "Super Tuesday" and will have very good leads in the delegate race.

I then will continue to run a great ad campaign, ground game, and overall campaign and will win many more primaries and caucuses until eventually clinching the Republican nomination sometime between April and May.

Chapter Ten
Future Debates And
Quorums

"An investment in knowledge pays the best interest." -Benjamin Franklin

---

After having a fairly good performance in the first debate, I will go into future debates with a little bit of momentum. I will stay steady in the top 3 in polling until the first primary or caucus. My numbers will go down a little bit but I will still be in third after I lose in the first primary or caucus. After the second primary or caucus, I will move up to second and come the fourth primary or caucus, I will narrowly be in first. I then will hold this momentum into "Super Tuesday" attacking my challenger in all ways I can on the debate stage.

I will widen the gap more and more by running more and more adds and doing more and more good performances in debates and quorums and will eventually clinch the nomination. I will be in the public eye during almost all of the debates and the battle for the nomination will be ruthless, but I will prevail.

Chapter Eleven
Getting The Nomination

"It's a damn poor mind indeed which can't think
of at least two ways to spell any word."
-Andrew Jackson

It will take a lot of effort to win the nomination,
but I will do it. Countless rallies will need to be
held in key states, but you must do more than
hold a rally. You must engage with the voters if
you are to win.

As I said before, I believe I will lose the first
primary or caucus. I believe I will get about
23% of the vote in the primary or caucus and
will get some delegates. I'm going to totally
make up a schedule that has been similar in
previous years to base what I am about to say
from. No matter what the schedule is, I will get
the nomination. This schedule is just a
hypothetical situation with results I believe I will
be able to achieve, but we'll see in 2040.

Schedule
Date, State Caucus/Primary, Delegates
Available, Delegates I Will Win
February 1, Iowa Caucus, 33, 8

February 7, New Hampshire Primary, 18, 6
February 18, South Carolina Primary, 33, 33
February 28, Nevada Caucus, 30, 12
March 6, Alaska Caucus, 28, 9
March 6, Arkansas Primary, 37, 13
March 6, Georgia Primary, 75, 26
March 6. Massachusetts Primary, 42, 13
March 6, Minnesota Caucus, 36, 10
March 6, Oklahoma Primary, 41, 11
March 6, Tennessee Primary, 56, 24
March 6, Vermont Primary, 17, 7
March 6, Virginia Primary, 49, 16
March 10, Kansas Caucus, 41, 15
March 10, Louisiana Primary, 45, 20
March 13, Alabama Primary, 48, 21
March 13, Hawaii Caucus, 20, 9
March 13, Mississippi Primary, 40, 19
March 20, Florida Primary, 70, 70
March 20, Illinois Primary, 67, 27
March 20, Missouri Primary, 54, 25
March 20, North Carolina Primary, 62, 30
March 27, Arizona Primary, 44, 44
March 27, Ohio Primary, 65, 40
March 27, Utah Caucus, 40, 40
April 10, Wisconsin Primary, 41, 14
April 10, Michigan Primary, 45, 29
April 10, Maryland Primary, 37, 37
April 10, Texas Primary, 150, 85

April 14, Colorado Convention, 30, 0
April 24, New York Primary, 95, 75
April 24, Connecticut Primary, 28, 20
April 24, Delaware Primary, 16, 13
April 24, Pennsylvania Primary, 45, 45
April 24, Rhode Island Primary, 18, 7
May 1, Indiana Primary, 52, 52
May 1, West Virginia, 31, 20
May 8, Oregon Primary, 26, 12
May 8, Nebraska Caucus, 35, 25
May 15, Washington Primary, 42, 26
May 22, California Primary, 172, 125
May 22, Montana Caucus, 26, 19
May 22, New Jersey Primary, 50, 50
May 22, New Mexico Primary, 25, 19
May 22, South Dakota Primary 27, 23
May 22, Wyoming Caucus, 29, 24
May 22, Idaho Caucus, 33, 27
May 22, North Dakota Caucus, 28, 25

Chapter Twelve
The Convention

"As it is an ancient truth that freedom cannot
be legislated into existence, so it is no less
obvious that freedom can not be censored into
existence" -Dwight D. Eisenhower

The 2040 Republican National Convention
should be held at The Palace of Auburn Hills in
Auburn Hills, Michigan. I will be officially
nominated there at some point between July
and August of 2040. The convention will last
four days, as usual, and there will be many
guest speakers. It will be a great opportunity to
showcase what the party has to offer that year.

I will give a speech at the convention on the
last day of the convention. Below is the likely
transcript of that speech.

"Thank you, thank you. Everyone here tonight
watching and in the crowd, I have one thing to
say: I accept your nomination for President of
the United States! *crowd cheers*

I have all of you to thank for this great honor.

It took a great fight to get here, but I am willing to fight for the rest of my days for this country and you the people. I have been fighting for the people since 2022, and I would gladly do it again if I was given the opportunity.

Tonight I am asking all of you, even those who didn't vote for me, to stand in solidarity with our great movement. This is not a political party issue. This is a common sense issue. We have many problems that we are facing, and my opponent absolutely can not solve them. They have no chance. Zero. I am also asking you to join us on the journey to prosperity.

Under my administration, we will be a nation of prosperity where you the people matter and we the people take back control of our government. For far too long have the Washington insiders run the game, and that game was established to be against you. We must unite against this. I vow to every American tonight that I will fight against the elite who control our government.

Last night you heard a speech from my Vice Presidential pick. I think he is a fantastic person and will work side by side with us to help us seek something better.

We will seek something better in education. We are ranked 14th worldwide in education. When is it ever acceptable to come in 14th place? We as a country are the greatest in the world, our leaders however are not. They are to blame for our horrible rankings in education. We will fix this with a few steps.

Step one is to change the outdated schedule. The whole system is outdated. We're going to change the system requirements, and let local government decide the rest. Education works best when run locally. We will implement a 4-3 system where students must go to school for four days then get three days off. We're also going to raise the mandatory amount of days you must go to school each year to 210 from 180.

Step two is to is to reform the amount of classes you must take. We will eliminate the 12th grade and replace it with mandatory preschool nationwide. Studies find that if children don't receive early brain stimulation, they will not excel educationally in the future.

This is why it will be mandatory to go to preschool in the USA.

Finally, step three is to end property tax based education. Lots of states rely on property taxes to fund education but since wealthy houses are worth more, they pay more in property taxes. This means that the wealthy zip codes get better schools and typically a better education than the rest of America. It will vary by states and be up to the states to determine the amount, but the amount of money that funds public education will need to be flat. If California collects $100 million and has 100 zip codes, each zip code gets $1 million in funding. Too long have the elite benefited from the rest of us. No longer will this happen, especially in our educational system. Overall, the educational system in America under my administration will thrive, and will certainly be better than it is right now.

We will seek something better in our tax system. For years, the tax system has been disproportionate. Even the solutions to our current tax system are disproportionate. This is why we will have a 20% flat tax rate. We will also make sure the elite do not exploit our tax system by eliminating all deductions and loopholes currently available and currently used by many. Every four years we will also have a total tax vacation in which no one pays any federal income tax. It will be amazing for all of us and the economy.

We will seek something better in the Federal Reserve. I did not release my plan for the Federal Reserve yet, and what better time is there to do so? We are going to End the monopoly of banks known as the Federal Reserve. The Federal Reserve, created in 1913, has caused the value of the dollar to lose a little over 95% of it's value. In 1913, for $4.10, you could buy $100 worth of stuff. The reason the money is worth less is because the more money there is in existence, the less each bill is worth.

The Federal Reserve is a debt machine. The Federal Reserve is responsible for over $2.5 trillion of our National Debt. The way the system works is that whenever the government wants money, the issue treasury bonds. These treasury bonds are then sold to the Federal Reserve in exchange for "Federal Reserve Notes", or dollars. These dollars were created out of thin air and have no value whatsoever. You see, they used to have value. You used to be able to turn in you ten dollar bill for ten dollars worth of gold. Those slips of paper had actual value. Now, what's a piece of paper worth?

Anyways, the U.S. must pay interest on the money they borrowed from the Fed, the only problem is this: If you borrowed the first dollar into existence but promised to pay it back, plus interest, how do you pay it back? You can't! You must continuously borrow.

The whole system is a scam and the banks make billions in profits each year from it. We will lend it entirely. It will be replaced with a system much much better, one where actual things of value are used as currency. Both gold and silver will be used as currency in the U.S. The U.S. Treasury will print our money now, so no National Debt is added while printing and the process is interest free. The money can be redeemed by all for either the value in gold or silver. The gold or silver can also be redeemed at any time for it's value in dollars, and so on. We will print a limited amount of dollars each year due to the fact they must be backed by a limited amount of gold and silver. This will stop us from mass producing dollars at the expense of devaluing our currency and creating debt. There is a problem, and it will be solved.

America will always solve the problems it is facing. No longer will we allow problems to build up and become bigger ones, or even develop in the first place. Patient diplomacy is a synonym for doing nothing.

We will seek something better in foreign policy. We will be anti-interventionist 100%. 100%. With my opponent, you would get involved in many useless wars. We will lead America back to prosperity rather than Iraq back to poverty at the cost of $2.4 trillion and thousands of lives. If another country is in a civil war, we will let them sort out their problems. The only time we as a nation will get involved is if we are threatened, both verbally and literally. We do not tolerate disrespect of our great nation. Patriotism will rise once again under my administration.

We will also cut foreign aid in half and will cut troop levels worldwide in half. They will train here in the U.S. until they are needed. This doesn't mean that we will not improve our military. We will have a military so strong that we don't have to use it rather than one so weak that we can't use it. I will increase military spending and get much more out of the spending than we currently do.

We will seek something better in immigration. Illegal immigration is a problem, and we must solve it. Each year, at the state local and federal level, illegal immigration costs taxpayers about $113 billion. In no other country in the world can you break the country's laws and be rewarded.

Most illegals don't pay taxes. Some do, most don't. Less than 50% of illegals pay taxes. Most the money they pay into taxes, about $12 billion, they get back. In addition, the amount they pay in taxes is just about 10% of their cost. They certainly aren't paying for everything they get.

Illegals who don't pay taxes will be deported, effective immediately. Illegals in our prisons will be deported as well. Illegals who pay taxes and have no criminal record will be given a choice: be escorted out of the country and come back in legally and get full citizenship or immediately get permanent residency. With permanent residency, you are not given the right to vote. You lose the right to vote when you come here illegally. If they decide to leave and come back, they will get the right to vote as they will become citizens.

We will change the laws regarding legal immigration to this country as well. The U.S. will cap the amount of people it accepts into the U.S. each year at 0.15% of the U.S. population at the last census. Those who decide to leave the country and come back in legally will not be counted on this tally. We will also change the amount of time you can stay on the waiting list without reply to one year. Within one year of your filing for citizenship, you will get a response. Finally, we will implement a queue system in which those who can contribute more get accepted first. No longer will it be first come first serve. If there was someone with a college education applying for citizenship and someone without one applying, the one with a college education will get accepted first.

Now, back to illegal immigration. Here are some statistics for everyone. In 2014, about 50% of federal crimes were committed near the U.S. Mexico border. Also, in 2014, illegals accounted for about 75% of federal drug sentences. About 50% of illegals came from Mexico. This is why we will secure the Mexico-U.S. border with enhanced new security. The cost of this new security will be about $11.3 billion per year. This is in addition to the current amount spent. This $11.3 billion is 10% of the amount illegals cost us each year. Also, since the $11.3 billion prevents illegal immigration, it saves money. I'm not done with the statistics. About 8% of the illegal population is in prison as opposed to about 0.8% of the legal population. There are a mere 1,000 illegal Americans in Mexico as opposed to about 6 million illegal Mexicans in the U.S. and believe me, you don't get the same benefits as an illegal in Mexico. Illegals account for 5%-30% of convictions for murder and rape despite representing a mere 3.5% of the U.S. population.

If we removed every single illegal immigrant by deportation it would cost about $500 billion. It takes less than 5 years for the U.S. to spend this amount of money on illegals. I won't do this though because some of them are good people. Some are criminal tax evaders but some actually are good.

Overall, illegal immigration in my administration will be a thing of the past. We will begin the deportation of the bad illegals on my first day in office and will begin the process of permanent residency or citizenship on the first day as well. Legals will be able to come to the U.S. legally and the best will get to enter the best country in the world first!

Finally, we will seek something better in Social Security. Social Security is a system that accounts for $2.8 trillion of debt. This is about 14% of our national debt. This money is owed to the trust fund by the U.S. Treasury, but in order for the treasury to get money, they must create more debt.

You might be wondering why this money is owed. Well, the answer is that the government wasted it, or stole from we the people. The money was spent on wars and other government programs. Your stolen money was wasted.

Social Security takes 6.2% out of your paycheck each year and in return, on average, gives you about $16,000 each year. This is a mere $4,300 above the poverty line, and that poverty line is for single people. If married, that poverty line is $16,000, or the average benefit received.

According to Gallup, 33.3% of Americans have no retirement savings and therefore will be forced to live slightly above or at the poverty line. This however is right now. By 2034, benefits are estimated to be cut 23%. This means the average annual benefit will reach $12,300. Now, if you are single, you are $500 over the poverty level and if you are married, you are $3,700 below the poverty level, and this is just 17 years from now. Imagine what our current 18 year olds will get when they retire.

Don't worry, I have a solution to this devastating problem. If we made it law that employers must put 3.7% of your annual salary into a retirement savings account, and assumed you made the average salary in America of about $45,000, you would make $3,375 a month for retirement instead, at about

⅓ of the cost. The best part is it is no cost to you the people, the cost in solely on the employer's and believe me, this is no burden to them. They make astronomical profits, and that's ok, but this won't put them out of business. This system will be implemented whenever the last American who has put money into Social Security dies. This new program won't be able to be implemented until years from now, but it will be a great change for the country and the system as a whole. I also swear to all seniors that I will attempt to increase your monthly pensions.

Political divisiveness has ruined our country. Lots of people simply listen and obey to what their party leaders say they should do, especially those on the other side. They ignore the facts or call them or yourself key phrases like "racist", "fascist", or "conspiracy theorists". Some of these people will defend their party or their leaders no matter what they do. It's horrible. I am reaching beyond all of the party lines and trying to get every American's vote. I am not tied to the Republicans or the Democrats, I am tied to you the people.

I will restore an era of victory and prosperity into our nation. We are going to eliminate the entire national debt within eight years if we are given the chance to. The only way for this to happen is for all of you to go out and vote on November 6th!

The American dream has been destroyed by Washington. Washington has regulated and taxed the incentives out of all of us. Companies put their jobs over in China, fire their employees, and expect no consequences. Americans for years have been wanting to seek something better, but there was nothing in sight. I have laid out plans that will bring back the American dream and will restore the legacy of greatness in America, a legacy that has been absent for decades.

We deserve better, and I will give you better. America has been mocked by the world for years. America has been full of poverty. For years America has been defeated. It is time to bring America back to victory, and bring our people along with us.

In our America, the America in which we the people are in charge and our country is a free and safe nation with free and safe markets, we are the superpower of the world. Right now we are not. If we would like the heart of our nation that beats the blood of patriots to be restored, then you must go out ad vote, go out and volunteer, go out and help our movement be a successful one and help us seek something better! Our country will be made so much better with your help. We the people will seek something better and restore prosperity in America! Thank you, thank you all, god bless you and god bless the USA!

Chapter Thirteen
The General Election Rallies

"Whenever you do a thing, act as if all the world were watching." -Thomas Jefferson

---

My general election rallies will be amazing. They will attract thousands of people each time. I will hold about 2 rallies per day between July and September and then in the months of October and November, I will hold about 4 rallies per day. Locations of the rallies will vary by polling but I will hold rallies in all 50 states, as I did in the primaries, and my goal this time will be to attract 75,000 people at at least one rally in each state, even though in some states I should be able to attract over 100,000 supporters.

Overall, these rallies will help me get elected and engage with and attract voters. These rallies will be very energetic and patriotic. At this point, I will have people from across the political spectrum joining our movement and attending the amazing rallies that will help us seek something better!

Chapter Fourteen
The Presidential Debates

"I believe that banking institutions are more dangerous to our liberties than standing armies. If the American people ever allow private banks to control the issue of their currency, first by inflation, then by deflation, the banks and corporations that will grow up around the banks will deprive the people of all property until their children wake-up homeless on the continent their fathers conquered."
-Thomas Jefferson

The three presidential debates should take place in October of 2040. These debates will be used by me to totally derail my opponent's campaign. My rallies will be when I speak of policies and the debates will be spent explaining why my opponent's policies are bad and why mine are better. I will not have any sort of slip up in these debates and will go in with a very good record. I will also try my best to get supporters of mine in the audience and for people to view the debates on my social media pages. Overall, these debates will help my campaign by hurting my opponent's indefinitely. All opposition will be defeated.

The Stance To Get Elected

The Stance To Get Elected

Chapter Fifteen
The Ad Campaign

"Everyone wants to live at the expense of the state. They forget that the state wants to live at the expense of everyone." -Frederic Bastiat

---

My ad campaign will be essential to my election. Initially, prior to the primaries, my ads will just speak about me, my views, and information on the campaign.

Getting closer to the primaries, I will begin on of the greatest stream of attack ads America has ever seen. Throughout the primaries my ads will vary but again, due to massive amounts of funds, they will air all day every day and will be very effective.

The same goes for during the general election. During this, I will instruct my communications director to create a new ad every day. I will pay for this and airtime for four hours each day of these ads, always between 5PM and 8PM. These ads will vary by state but I would say around four ads a week will be attack ads and three ads per week will be ads supporting myself, my ideas, and our movement.

The Stance To Get Elected

Chapter Sixteen
Election Day

"Liberty cannot be preserved without general knowledge among the people." -John Adams

---

November 6th, 2040 is election day. People across America will go out and vote, and hopefully it will be for me. There should be about 155 million people who vote that election, according to census data and turnout rates. I believe I could get anywhere from 50%-60% of these votes. I also believe I could hit about 330 electoral votes.

Assuming I am victorious, my victory speech will occur at the Wells Fargo Center in Pennsylvania, but either way I will appear here on election night.

Chapter Seventeen
Victory Speech

"Those who stand for nothing fall for anything."
-Alexander Hamilton

Assuming that I win the election on November 6th, 2040, here is a likely transcript of my victory speech.

"Thank you, thank you.

Our opponent has conceded, we are victorious.

Tonight is a historic night in the face of the United States and the world. It also is a historic night for those who are attempting to rule over us like dictators as they will never gain access to our great country again. We have defeated the monopoly they have, and we will destroy that very monopoly.

Our country will solve the problems we are facing, and we are facing many problems, but we will do so as a country, not just as myself or Congress or any single individual. You voted me into this position to lead so now I will lead in this position for you the people.

The Stance To Get Elected

I vow to every American tonight that I will fight for and alongside you.

Whether you voted for me or not, I will represent you. I will represent the United States of America as a whole. I will restore the legacy of prosperity into America the likes of which has not been seen since Andrew Jackson, 2 centuries ago.

We the people have just taken back control of the government. This hard fought battle was fought not to elect me but to fix our great country to restore the American dream, to bring money and jobs back, to fix the tax system, to fix our whole country, together as one nation, under god.

I will destroy party lines, and I will do it for we the people. For too long has our country been divided. Whether it was the North and the South, the federalists or the anti-federalists, or the Republicans or the Democrats, they all divided our country. They forced us to not live or believe by choice but rather believe in what party leaders tell us to believe in. You know you are doing something good when the elite

The Stance To Get Elected

don't like or support you. We have been challenged by the elite because they know we are going to end their monopoly and give the power to all Americans. With that being said, I don't care if you have lots of money, that doesn't ,matter. I don't care if you are greedy, that is essential. What I care about, and you should to, is the fact that some of these elitists control, literally control, the gears of our government.

We're pro capitalism, capitalism is an unequal amount of wealth while socialism and communism are equal amounts of poverty. No socialist country has succeeded in any way better than capitalist nations. Socialism always fails in the end. Capitalism has it's small amount of flaws but no system is perfect, and capitalism is the greatest economic system to ever be developed throughout the history of the world.

We the country will work together to seek something better. We will do so all over the country. I can tell you one thing, as a matter of fact I will promise this: by the end of my first term, your life will be better than it is right now. I also pledge I won't spend my first term trying to get elected a second, although I believe I will get elected a second term and doing so would allow me to finalize on my policies that are the best, like ending the national debt.

Traveling around the country, our movement drew hundreds, thousands, tens of thousands, and even at points over 100,000 people. Turnout for voting was much higher than this. During this experience, i've gotten to know what all of you must go through and what you all believe in and want. I have formed the largest bond in my life with this country and it's people. This bond is so great as I believe in and love this country. I love this country not because it's perfect, it surely isn't. I love this country because everyone has the potential to be what they are willing to work for. These opportunities aren't just given to the people in terms of jobs, they are given to us in the form of new political figures with new policies.

Our policies will drastically improve our ways of life and our country as a whole, and remember, never forget this: we will seek something better. Thank you everyone, thank you all, god bless you and the United States."

Chapter Eighteen
The Background

"We have a system that increasingly taxes work and subsidizes nonwork."
-Milton Friedman

I should get elected as governor of Pennsylvania in 2034. If I am to get elected to this position, I will need to have a solid background. Prior to this, I will have been a member of the House of Representatives in Pennsylvania's 10th congressional district for 2 terms, mayor of Williamsport, Pennsylvania, a city council member in Williamsport, Pennsylvania, and I will have graduated from Penn State with a degree in political science.

Overall, Pennsylvania will be my new home state, the people there will love me, and I will have a great record of being a public servant in the past so that I can get elected in 2034 for Governor of Pennsylvania.

Chapter Nineteen
The Announcement

"Live as if you were to die tomorrow. Learn as if you were to live forever." -Mahatma Gandhi

---

My announcement speech will be held on May 1st, 2033. It could be held in many different places but the most likely place in which it will be held is at Howard J Lamade Stadium in Williamsport, Pennsylvania. The announcement speech should get about 3,500 to attend. The speech will be about 2,500 words and will take about 45 minutes to give. Below is a likely transcript of that very speech.

"Thank you all, thank you very much. Let me start off by saying thank you to all of Williamsport who made it possible for me to be here today. Words cannot express how thankful I am for you guys.

Let me also state that today is the beginning of a great journey. I am running for governor of Pennsylvania!

Our great state of Pennsylvania is being overrun and overruled by people that honestly dont give a damn about you. They don't. I however do.

Our leaders in Pennsylvania have created a $130 billion debt. Do you have any idea how much money this is? It would take our city of Williamsport 240 years to earn that much money. 240 years. It is insane.

I will decrease the deficit in Pennsylvania by the end of my first term and will create a surplus each year on our budget.

On the subject of money, let's look at our state's economy. I like the way we are taxed, it's a flat tax. I however don't like the amount. I cut our tax rate from 3.07% to 2.5%. This is about 20% reduction in the rate. Our corporate income tax rates are also extremely high, the second highest in the U.S. to be exact. We will change this to the second lowest in the U.S. We will cut the corporate tax rate to 5% from 10%. If we don't, our people will continuously be unemployed as they have been for years and companies will abandon us. We don't want that do we? We are in the bottom 30% of states in terms of employment rates. 70% of states have a lower unemployment rate than us. In 4 out of the 5 states with the lowest unemployment rates, the corporate tax rate is less than 5%. By the end of my first term, Pennsylvania's unemployment rate will be less than what the U.S. unemployment rate is.

I will also encourage employment by offering a 0.1% tax deduction per 2,000 employees. We will also offer new businesses a tax free first year. This will encourage the development of small businesses and help them grow. New companies that come here to the state of Pennsylvania will also get benefits. Every new plant with 1,000 or more workers built in my administration will receive a 1% tax deduction. Our state will no longer tax businesses out of business. Instead, we will support business and the employment of workers, and overall our economic situation as a whole will be much better off than it is right now.

Crime is actually at OK levels in our state. We have the 23rd highest level. I'd like this to go down to 26th, so that way the majority of states have higher crime rates than us, and that really is the only goal I have for crime rates in our state. If something isn't broken, why would we try to fix it?

The Stance To Get Elected

Don't let these crime numbers fool you. This is about the only good thing that has come from our leaders, and even the crime levels aren't that astonishing. Most states have lower crime rates. Our government is very inefficient and absolutely does not represent you, as it should. Most voters in our state are registered as Democrats, but that means nothing to me. I have always ran as a Republican but I have never been one. Unfortunately, you can not run as a n indepent successfully or a Libertarian successfully and therefore I choose the Republican party. Yes, I have Republican beliefs but I also have independent beliefs, Libertarian beliefs, and at times Democratic beliefs. I will reach beyond party lines, as I don't identify with any political party, and will do what is best for the people and the state of Pennsylvania, not what is best for the special interest groups.

For too long have Pennsylvanians dealt with crumbling roads, bridges, airports, highways, dams, and overall infrastructure. Act 89 was a step in the right direction but absolutely wasn't enough. 25% of our bridges are structurally deficient, 25% of our dams have high hazard potential, water spread outbreaks are on the rise. While we're on water, let me talk about water fluoridation real quick. Water fluoridation is the only drug forced on the medication with no dosage control. Dozens and dozens of studies have linked water fluoridation to brain damage, and we will repeal the law that makes it illegal to remove fluoridation from our water supply. Ok, now back to infrastructure. Our inland waterways are 150 years old. When they were built, we were fighting in the civil war. They are so old. Our roads are just crumbling and the whole situation is a mess. I will fix it as much as I can in ten years by putting forward $5 billion each year to infrastructure spending. I believe with this large sum of money, I along with other members of government can fix the huge problem regarding infrastructure. If you are to remember one policy from my speech, remember this: I will not add one penny to the state debt.

Immigration will also be enforced in Pennsylvania. Federal laws have made it clear that we must obey their laws in regards to immigration. We have 18 sanctuary cities in Pennsylvania. This is the same amount they have in California. This is absurd! We will end all sanctuary cities in our state and let the federal government remove who they believe they should remove, but we will not aid criminals/foreigners, that is the definition of treason. In about half of the states in the U.S., there are no sanctuary cities. We will become one of those states as well in 2034!

Education in Pennsylvania is OK in the K-12 level. We are 12th in the U.S. in K-12. We however our the worst state in the country for higher education the worst. Pennsylvania should never be last in anything, ever. Yet here we are. We will fix the schedule in Pennsylvania for K-12 education as well as the funding for higher education. We drastically fund K-12 education in preparation for college but hardly do anything for college. You can prepare as much as you want for a battle but you still have no control of that battle. This is how it is right now in terms of education.

The K-12 schedule will be changed so that we have a 4-3 system. Four days of school and then 3 days off. This system will go on for however many days local governments want, as long as students attend school for at least 200 days each year.

In terms of higher education, we will drastically increase the budget. We will raise the budget for higher education to $750 million from $450 million. Now, with that being said, simply giving more money to the system doesn't help. Throwing money at a trashcan doesn't make it perform any better. I am not an educator and I have nothing to do with that area, so I will appoint and instruct a great individual to lead the Department of Education back to prosperity, as well as higher education. Education will be great in my administration and failed education will be a thing of the past.

I'm not sure if I've said it enough yet, so I'll say it again: I will not add a penny to the state debt. Not one cent, and as a matter of fact, I will create a surplus each year. I will lower the income tax rate to 2.5% flat. I will end the death and estate tax, end the tire fee, raise cigarette tax to $5 per pack from $2.6, raise liquor tax from 18% to 20%, cut corporate tax rate from 10% to 5%, cut vehicle lease and rent taxes in half, and cut sales tax from 6% to 5%. The total revenue from all of this will be about $35 billion. Pennsylvania will spend approximately $34.99 billion each year, generating a surplus on the budget that will be put towards a rainy day fund. I, unlike most other governors, will help end the state debt. My opponents will just increase it even more and then eventually stick you with the bill. Horrible.

Socially, I am pretty center, and overall I am a libertarian. I believe the second amendment shouldn't tampered with even more than it is right now, and I believe concealed carry of handguns should be legalized statewide without a need for permits. The second amendment is your permit, and it never expires! States like Alaska and Vermont allow this, and they have one of the lowest gun crime rates.

On abortion, I believe it should be avoided at all costs, but I will obey the Supreme Court and allow it to be the women's choice, but this choice will have limitations. I do not have the right to kill a human with fully developed organs and tissues, a heartbeat, brain waves, and feelings, and neither should anyone else. Babies can feel pain at 10 weeks, have fully functioning organs at 8 weeks, have brain waves measured at about 8 weeks, and develop a heartbeat at week 3. For this reason, we will ban abortion after 12 weeks, or 3 months. Right now, in our state, abortion is banned after 6 months, but at this point a baby is already yawing, feeling pain, and has a consciousness. A consciousness! It feels the knife going into the back of it's neck and knows it is dying! It's sick! Again, I'm fine with you getting an abortion, the law of the land is that it's legal. Murder is however illegal, and killing a conscious being with brainwaves, a heartbeat, and fully functioning organs is murder.

On free speech, I, along with almost everyone, am a strong advocate for it. I don't believe any of our taxpayer dollars should be spent on censoring free speech or regulate how we communicate via social media, or in any way. Our state representatives have been passing anti free speech legislation for years now. It's insanity! Under my administration, we will spend none of your money on censorship or regulation of your constitutional rights.

Electing me will be a total takeover of our government! We the people will have total control of the government. No longer will the incentives be taxed out of us, will we censor free speech, will we allow murder of babies, will we add money to the state debt, will we advocate for gun control, which is the very reason we have gun related deaths, will we have schools that rank in last, and no longer will we discourage patriotism.

We the people will take back our government in a revolution unlike anything they have ever seen before! We the people of Pennsylvania will end the lies, thank you, god bless you all, thank you very much!"

Chapter Twenty
The Primary

"Loyalty to country always. Loyalty to government, when it deserves it." -Mark Twain

---

I will run for governor of Pennsylvania in 2034. I believe I will have one or two challengers on the Republican side but that is it. The primary will occur sometime in May of 2034. I believe I will get around 50% of the vote in the primary. This will be more than any other candidate running for governor as a Republican. I will win the primary and will therefore go on to the general election in which I will face my opponent(s).

Chapter Twenty One
The Ad Campaign

""A paranoid is someone who knows a little of what's going on. " -William Burroughs

---

Ads are the key to victory, especially when you are a very unknown one term governor, one term member of city council, and two term member of the house. I will release a new ad every other day in every county in Pennsylvania that will air at primetime on local channels. This will attract the necessary amounts of voters needed to get the nomination and become governor. About 75% of these ads will be attack ads. If you obliterate the other candidate and their reputation, voters only have one other choice: you. Of course, I will also have positive ads about myself. I will have a member of my staff known as the ad director who will help determine what should be in these ads, who to target, when to air the ads, and so on. My ad campaign will be very good, very successful, and very essential to winning the race in 2034.

Chapter Twenty Two
Election Day

"I predict future happiness for Americans, if they can prevent the government from wasting the labors of the people under the pretense of taking care of them." -Thomas Jefferson

---

On November 7, 2034, Pennsylvanians will be able to choose the fate of their great state. They could choose a path of prosperity or a path of continuation and a path of failure. I will have an event planned that night in which I will deliver a speech, and this speech should be a victory speech.

Going into election day, I will have bombarded voters with advertisements and will have a fairly large lead in the polls. I will become the next governor of Pennsylvania in 2034 and will deliver a victory speech on the night of November 7 as voters join me in celebration of our successful movement.

Chapter Twenty Three
Victory Speech

"The heaviest penalty for declining to rule is to be ruled by someone inferior to yourself."
-Plato

On November 7, 2034, I will have officially been elected by the people as governor of Pennsylvania. That night, I will deliver a victory speech from the Hersheypark Arena in Hershey, Pennsylvania. Below is a likely transcript of that speech.

"Wow, thank you. Thank you.

Well, it's official: we won. With less funds and less recognition, we have defeated the establishment. You are the reason we won. Countless amounts of you volunteered and helped me get elected and even more of you went out and voted, and I thank you for that.

Today is the beginning of a new era in Pennsylvania. This era will no longer allow the unemployment rate to be higher than the federal unemployment rate. We will no longer tax the incentives out of both individuals and companies. We will no longer be ranked last in anything, especially education. We will lower the state debt. We will no longer allow our infrastructure to crumble and will no longer fund useless projects that we get hardly nothing out of.

You the people voted to end the lies, and that is exactly what we will do. We have been lied to all of our lives by the establishment. We have been lied to and fooled by them for far too long. Promises have been made but those promises have not been kept. We are different. I saw what was happening to our great state and I realized that I had to do something about it and fix it. Fixing something requires big moves, and I am willing to make those moves, unlike others. These moves will always be in the best interest of our state, not in the best interest of the special interest groups.

Because of you the people, our system is going to be fixed. I will lead our state to prosperity and I will bring you along with me, but I couldn't do anything without you all.

Remember, you are given 100% of the credit for our great and now successful movement.

The Stance To Get Elected

This movement is devoted to ending the failed policies that have ruined our state. We took the initiative to fix our state, and believe me, we will fix it. We will fix it for all of us.

Ever since our state was founded, it was time to end the lies. Today marks the beginning of that process. Thank you all, god bless you, thank you!"

Chapter Twenty Four
Get Politically Involved

"Freedom is never more than one generation away from extinction. We didn't pass it to our children in the bloodstream. It must be fought for, protected, and handed on for them to do the same, or one day we will spend our sunset years telling our children and our children's children what it was once like in the United States where men were free."

You yourself don't have to run for elected office to be politically involved. All you have to do is vote, but it is much better if you volunteer for candidates that align with your views.

Whether you are a Republican, Democrat, Libertarian, Independent, or whatever, you must use your vote to let your voice be heard. If you do not vote, you lose your voice and should not complain about political issues due to the fact you didn't vote to change it. Even if your candidate loses, you still will have used your voice.

Also, never ever think that you shouldn't vote for a candidate because it seems like the candidate will lose. Wouldn't you rather vote for someone who you think is right and lose than vote for someone who you don't like and then have them win?

You would be surprised at how many people are not politically involved or even politically informed. Here is some information gathered from various polls:

- 36% of Americans can't name all three branches of government, and 35% of them couldn't name any of them. (Business Insider)
- 61% of Americans don't know what political party controls the House of Representatives. (Business Insider)
- 46% of Americans don't know the political party of their local representative. (Washington Post)
- 77% of American Millennials don't know any of the senators from their state. (Politico)
- 63% of Americans can't name a Supreme Court Justice.
- 33% of Americans can't name the Vice President. (Pew Research)
- 23% of Americans don't know we have a National Debt. (Pew Research)

If you are to help a candidate get elected, or you are trying to get elected, the number one thing to do is to inform voters. Nelson Mandela once stated "Education is the most powerful weapon which you can use to change the world." If you campaigned for a candidate, all you have to do sometimes is explain what may seem like simple facts to them.

If you want to get more involved than simply voting, you can get to know candidates that are running, go to town hall meetings, go to city council meetings, join a campaign, volunteer at campaign headquarters, attend rallies, organize rallies, donate to campaigns, get merchandise from candidates, volunteer at polling places, and if you think you have it in you, run for office. If that seems like a lot, then just vote, but vote as an informed citizen. Read political books, follow the news, and most importantly, know the consequences of electing the candidate you support. If you can't explain what will happen when the candidate gets elected or why you should vote for the candidate, then don't vote for that candidate. Finally, know that your vote matters as much as every other vote, and remember: seek something better.

Index